A POCKET GUIDE TO LONDON WORDS & PHRASES

So you don't look stupid
when trying to understand
Cockney rhyming slang

PREFACE

For most people who are not from London, Cockney rhyming slang sounds like another language and can be extremely confusing. While the full rhyming phrases are multiple words, usually only the first part is used in a sentence. Confused? This mini illustrated 'dictionary' of Cockney rhyming slang is here to rescue you.

CHEERS!

ADAM & EVE

Believe.

"I don't Adam & Eve it!"

ALAN WICKERS

Knickers.

"You've got your Alan Wickers in a twist again."

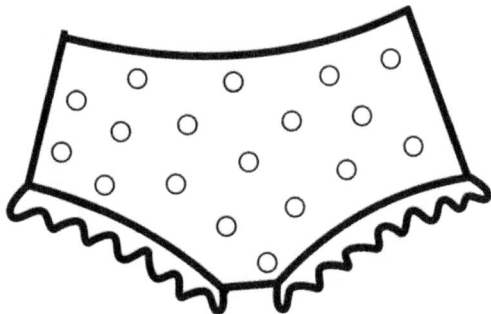

ALBERT HALL

Ball (testicles).

"He got on my nerves so I kicked him in the Alberts."

APPLES & PEARS

Stairs.

"Go up the apples and take a right."

ARMY & NAVY

Gravy.

"Pass the army and navy over here mum."

ARTFUL DODGER

Lodger.

"I've got an Artful in the spare room to help with the rent."

ASCOT RACES

Braces.

"He is now wearing Ascots."

BACARDI BREEZER

Freezer.

"I'll put the food in the bacardi."

BACON & EGGS

Legs.

"You have a lovely pair of bacons."

BAKED BEAN

Queen.

> "The speech at Christmas will never be
> the same again without our baked
> bean."

BARNET FAIR

Hair.

"She's been to the hairdressers, look at her barnet now."

BARNEY RUBBLE

Trouble.

"Are you causing barney rubble again?"

BEES & HONEY

Money.

"He robbed me and took the bees."

BIRD LIME

Time (in prison).

"He's doing bird for fighting."

BOAT RACE

Face.

"Nice legs but shame about her boat."

BOB MARLEY

Charlie (cocaine)

"There's no Bob Marley allowed in this city."

BRASS BANDS

Hands.

"I called it a deal and shook him by the brass."

BUTCHER'S HOOK

Look.

"Let me have a butchers."

CALLARD & BOWSWERS

Trousers.

"You've stained your callards, again."

CHICKEN ORIENTAL

Mental.

"He went chicken oriental."

CHINA PLATE

Mate.

"Alright my old China?"

CHRISTIAN SLATER

Later.

"See you Slater."

CREAM CRACKERED

Knackered (tired).

"I'm cream crackered."

CURRANT BUN

Sun.

"The currant bun is feeling hot today."

CLAIRE RAYNERS

Trainers.

"Going to town to get some new Claire Rayners later."

CUSTARD & JELLY

Telly.

"His custard looks like a microwave."

DANNY MARR

Car.

"I'll give you a lift in the Danny."

DICKY BIRD

Word.

"He hasn't said a Dicky bird today."

DOG & BONE

Phone.

"Ring me on the dog when you get in."

DONKEY'S EARS

Years.

"I've had these for donkeys."

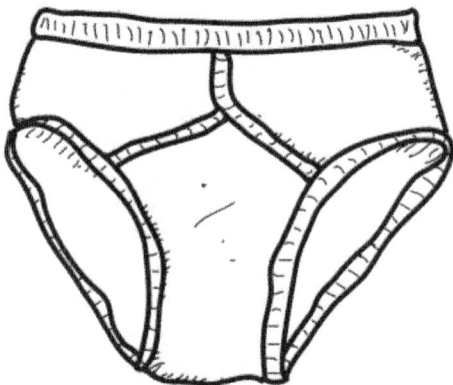

DRUM & BASE

Place (home).

"Meet me at my drum."

DUCK & DIVE

Hide.

"You need to duck n dive properly mate."

DUSTBIN LID

Kid.

"The dustbin lids are in school today."

ELEPHANT'S TRUNK

Drunk.

"He's elephant's trunk again."

FARMER GILES

Piles (hemorrhoids).

"My farmers are playing up today."

FISH TANK

Bank.

"I'll pay you back after I've been to the fish."

GREGORY PECK

Neck.

"Quick, get that down your gregory."

HALF INCH

Pinch (steal).

"Someone has half-inched my wallet."

HAMSTEAD HEATH

Teeth.

"I'll knock out your Hamstead Heath in a minute if you carry on."

HARRY MONK

Skunk (cannabis).

"I don't need any Harry Monk to have a good time."

HUCKLEBERRY FINN

PIN.

"I've forgotten my Huckleberry Finn."

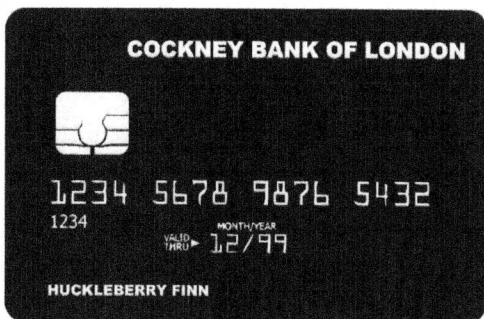

ITCH & SCRATCH

Match.

"Come and watch the itch with me."

JACK JONES

Own.

"I'm on my Jack Jones."

JIMMY FLINT

Skint.

"*I can't go for a drink tonight, I'm Jimmy Flint already.*"

JIMMY RIDDLE

Piddle (urinate).

"I need a Jimmy riddle."

KYBER PASS

Arse.

"Get your Khyber out of here."

LADY GODIVA

Fiver (£5 note).

"Got a Godiva on you mate?"

LEMON SQUEEZY

Easy.

"It was lemon mate."

LEMON TART

Smart.

"Don't get lemon with me."

LOAF OF BREAD

Head.

"Use your loaf for once before you speak."

MARS BAR

Scar.

"Where did you get that mars bar?"

MICKEY BLISS

Piss (mocking someone).

"He took the Mick out of him."

MINCE PIES

Eyes.

"Have a butchers with your mincers."

NEW DELHI

Belly.

"I've got a pain in my New Delhi."

NIGEL BEN

Ten.

"He owes me a Nigel."

NORTH & SOUTH

Mouth.

"She's got a really big north n south."

OILY RAG

Fag (cigarette).

"That was my last oily."

PEN & INK

Stink.

"Your socks pen and ink mate."

PETE TONG

Wrong.

"It's all gone Pete Tong."

PIG'S EAR

Beer.

"I owe you a pig's ear next time we go to the pub."

PLATE OF MEAT

Street.

"I was walking down the plate casually like this."

PLATES OF MEAT

Feet.

"I've been on my plates all day."

PONY & TRAP

Crap (talking sh*t).

"That's a load of pony mate."

PORK PIES

Lies (porkie pies).

"He was telling porkies when he said he won the lottery."

RABBIT & PORK

Talk.

"We'll have a good rabbit tomorrow."

RASPBERRY TART

Fart.

"Did you blow another raspberry?"

RATS & MICE

Dice (gambling).

"He's winning at the rats and mice again."

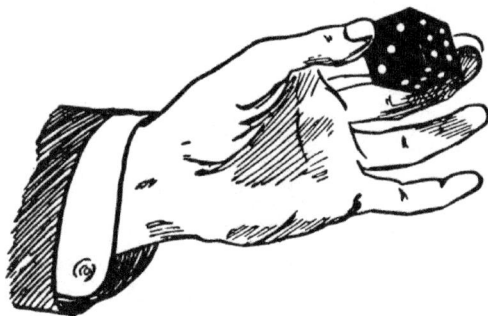

RICHARD THE THIRD

Turd.

"Dave is a complete Richard."

ROGER MOORE

Door.

"Close the Roger, it's freezing."

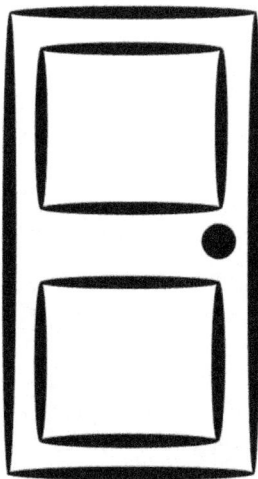

ROSY LEE

Tea.

> "Let's have a Rosy Lee and I'll tell you all about it."

RUB & DUB

Pub.

"I'll meet you at the rub n dub for a pint or few."

RUBY MURRAY

Curry.

"Fancy a Ruby tonight?"

SAUSAGE & MASH

Cash.

"Have you got any sausage and mash on you?"

SCOOBY DOO

Clue.

"I don't have a Scooby what time it is."

SEPTIC TANK

Yank (American).

"The septics across the pond won't have a clue what we're on about."

SHERBET DAB

Cab (taxi).

"I'm taking a sherbet."

SKIN & BLISTER

Sister.

"That's my skin n blister on the left."

SWEENEY TODD

Flying squad (police).

"Hurry up, here come the Sweeney."

SYRUP OF FIGS

Wig.

"Check out the syrup on his head."

TEA LEAF

Thief.

"Watch it, he's a tea leaf."

THREEPENNY BITS

Tits.

"Lovely threepenny bits."

TOM FOOLERY

Jewellery.

"That's some expensive looking Tom you have."

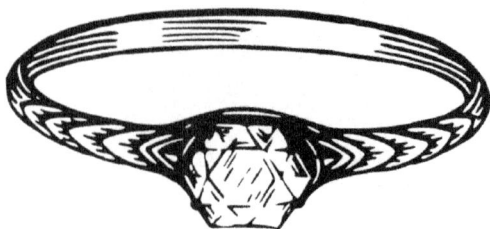

TREACLE TART

Sweetheart.

"Meet my treacle."

TROUBLE & STRIFE

Wife.

"Had an argument with the trouble again."

TURKISH BATH

Laugh.

"Are you having a Turkish mate?"

VERA LYNN

Gin.

"I'll have a shot of Vera."

WEASEL & STOAT

Coat.

"Put on your weasel, it's cold out there."

WEST HAM
RESERVES

Nerves.

"You're getting on my West Hams now."

WHISTLE & FLUTE

Suit.

"Looking smart in your new whistle."

Printed in Great Britain
by Amazon